Manic July

a poetry collection

casey marie

BookLeaf Publishing

India | USA | UK

Made with ❤ on the BookLeaf Publishing Platform
www.bookleafpub.in
www.bookleafpub.com

Dedication

i dedicate this book to anyone, diagnosed or not, who suffers from any type of mental illness. to those who struggle with accomplishing day-to-day tasks, to anyone who feels that just surviving the day is a win, and to those who haven't had a chance to have their stories told.

i dedicate this book to those who understand, and to those who don't.

i dedicate this book to my husband and my children, who have loved me through it all unconditionally.

Preface

hi there,

When I was diagnosed with bipolar 1 and borderline personality in my early 20's, I had no idea how to deal with it all. I wish someone had handed me a how-to guide on surviving it. Unfortunately, there was little information... and even less accounts of personal experiences of others going through similar symptoms. I have always felt like a shapeshifter, a chameleon, a stranger in my own body. I tried on many personalities, and a pharmacy worth of medications, but nothing was quite the right fit. I had no idea who I was a human, and I struggled to juggle my duties as a wife and new mother while dealing with a mental illness. It all became too overwhelming, and the result was like a pressure cooker exploding. When it all erupted, I destroyed everything and everyone in my path.

During the summer of 2021 I experienced the worst manic episode I've had to date, with months of complete disassociation. When I finally came out of it, and the dust from my destruction settled, I was left with a lot of unprocessed thoughts and feelings.

This is when I found poetry. After reading and being inspired by others who wrote beautiful words about hard things, I knew I had to write to start to heal myself. I am

not a poet, but my heart pleaded me to give it a place to
release everything I had been bottling up. Writing this
book (among other poems) has given me a safe place to
heal and untangle what I've been through.

These poems are just a collection of messy thoughts from
my messy life, they aren't perfectly worded, they don't
always rhyme, and hell, they might not even make any
sense. Regardless, I'm choosing to share them in hopes
that someone (you?) will take comfort in knowing they
aren't alone, and as a sign things will get better in time.

If you've ever felt broken, useless, misunderstood by the
people you love...

If you've ever been told to just "feel better", to pull
yourself up by your bootstraps, or that all your problems
can be solved with a little sunlight and fresh air...

Then this is for you. There is no quick fix, there's no
magic elixir. It takes time, hard work, and for me... a
great therapist.

These poems are dedicated to the manic summer of 2021,
to all the things I did and people I've hurt while living
life on autopilot.

trigger & content warning:
sexual assault, sexual content, adult themes, drug use,
language, addiction

*if you are sensitive, this is your warning

** I do not condone any of the behavior or actions in this

book, it is only a retelling of my personal experiences.
consequences to these behaviors may vary. proceed with
caution.

Acknowledgements

big thanks are in order:

to my husband and children; for always showing up,
even on the hard days, and loving me unconditionally
through them all
to my parents & aunt; for always supporting my dreams,
and raising me to be the best i can be
to my siblings; for listening to me whine all these years,
always answering the phone when i call, and telling me
the truth when i ask if my outfit looks bad
to my guardian angels; for rooting me on, even in spirit. i
hope i make you proud.

drunk

i'm drunk again
but not a drop of liquor
has danced with my tongue
tonight
i'm dizzy
unsteady
and just a little bit
out   of   control
my cheeks are flushed
palms all clammy
gripping the steering wheel
and there are stars
in my eyes

moon full
highway empty
and warm august air
lashes my hair across my face
blurring my vision
driving on autopilot
and my skin is buzzing
with electric
like a neon sign
in a dusty bar window

radio is loud
but the lyrics are a blur
and i don't know
which lane to be in...
fast
or
s l o w
so, fuck it...
i'll use both

i'm all alone out here
drunk again
on the thought
of you

rough landing

you dizzied me
with the scent of your skin
paralyzed me
to my core
when those ice blue eyes
locked with mine
my knees
turned to jelly
as we stood in the doorway
trying to steal
just one more kiss
even though we've said
"goodnight, for real this time"
at least a hundred times

you made my guts
feel twisted inside
they were oh, so shy
terrified of the moment
it was time to say
goodbye

so many things
i wanted to say,

but couldn't
my heart was too busy
hiding inside my mouth
words got stuck
behind clean teeth
and in between sweat covered sheets

so desperate
for approval,
your praise
and your attention.
when you told me
i should "fall for you"
i almost laughed
at the mention

never expected
my feet to get tangled
sending me falling
with my head over my heels
but now i lay
broken and mangled
at the bottom of the stairs

the crash left me in pieces
crumbles on the ground
scars forever carved into my skin

until my body
grows frail and thin
you weren't bothered
you didn't even care
and you weren't there
to help
     me
       up

vortex

in my darkest moments
in the night's deepest hours,
no rose can hold a thorn to me
i'm not that kind of flower.

i hardly recognize my face,
these demons look too much like me.
Hell is not what i expected,
it's too familiar of a place to be.
my reality starts blurring,
can't determine right from wrong
now my daydreams turn to nightmares,
once innocent and pure,
morphed into something sinister
the devil laughs and says to me,
there isn't any cure

filled with poison
a liquid death
but my aura draws you in
you're slowly drowning,
sinking down...
you don't know how to swim

i lure you in, my siren song
sweet nothings in your ear
seduce you with some promises
i never plan to keep,
suck you in and suffocate
sing a soothing lullaby
and put you right to sleep

i transform into
a cosmic wonder
too big for you to grasp
a shooting star, a supernova
a galaxy of constellations
you're blinded by the milky way
though you found
the other half to your soul
but i've fooled you once again,
tricked you with a pretty face
i'm just a dead black hole

if you get too close
i'll bury you deep inside
trapping you in the bowels of the beast
you'll try to claw
your way back out,
but not even light can escape me
anything and anyone

unfortunate enough to fall
in proximity
of my gravity
will be the end of us all

one day you'll be gone

i'm reclaiming all
my memories
slowly but surely
and one at a time

the song i played on repeat
that once reminded me
of things we used to do

the road i avoided
driving down
because it led me
straight to you

that shirt i wore
the last time you
undressed me

turns out,
that inside joke
we laughed about together
wasn't all that funny

it's taken awhile
and it doesn't always work,
but everyday
i'm recapturing
those little moments,
where you used to
always lurk

walking contradiction

i find it harder and harder
to decipher what was real
to the world
and what was real
in my head
they were quite often
in disagreement

when the things i said
and things i did
and thoughts i believed in
contradicted one another
it gave me the reputation
of being a liar

when everything i said i stood for
was met with an opposing action
i appeared unstable,
untrustworthy,
and fake
to everyone around me

i was known as the girl
who couldn't make up her mind

who says one thing,
then does another
i started to panic,
everyone around was finally starting to see
i had no idea who i was
or how to just be me

but what they couldn't see
deep down inside
the battle raging on
a constant war, the fight between
my heart,
my soul,
my brain
and *her*
and
me

over medicated

take your medication
don't you ever
miss a dose

still not feeling
quite yourself?
let's double,
no wait,
triple the amount
this antidote
will set you free
and if it doesn't
you'll come back
crawling on your knees

it's been a few months
or maybe even years
we still can't figure out
why you're not
feeling better, dear
they've been developing a cure
you'll be our test subject
read this short pamphlet
it will highlight the allure

but being a zombie
brain and body numb
is more acceptable
than being "crazy",
so, we'll keep you
tucked under our thumb

open wide
swallow this horse pill
be a good girl
even if it's against your own will
oh, and on your way out
don't forget
to stop at the receptionist
and pay your bill

gears

i felt myself start changing
did it happen fast or slow?
month after month
year after year
or just a moment ago?
my body split open
slimy guts on display
one by one
they were taken away
plucked from their home
set gently on ice
don't want them to die
but they are needed right now
it's not the right time
i panic thinking that they'll sew me up
leaving my cavity hollow, empty inside
looking back,
i wish that was the case
they were plotting something
much more sinister than
leaving nothing in their place
instead they filled me up
with parts and pieces
that belonged to someone else

like an antique clock
with cogs and knobs all broken
the damaged bits are discarded
brand new ones are installed
changed some hardware
shined it up, now it's good as new
back to ticking like it should
looks all the same to a stranger
but something is wrong,
the parts don't fit quite right
and gears are grinding together
frustration builds inside me
i'm boiling over with anger
i scream and cry
that something's off
but nobody believes me
i insist that i'm broken,
even though i look just fine
my outsides might appear the same,
but the insides...
are not mine

routine

nicotine for breakfast
opioids for lunch
cocaine sprinkled in between
to keep me rolling steady
a well-balanced diet
of highs and lows
wrap me in their arms
with comfort
just like a favorite teddy

until evening creeps into dark
and solace turns to nightmares
i cannot sleep but i'm not quite awake
i'm somewhere in the middle
brain on fire
muscles paralyzed with fear

my arms and legs are petrified
a thousand-year-old rock,
there's a scream outside
it's getting closer
and i thought i heard a knock.
a thief is breaking into my house
i hear the deadbolt turning

my family is hurt and they're probably all dead
but it's just the paranoia
i've lost my shit
and i can't breathe
i need to get a grip

tomorrow will come
the sun will rise
just like it always does
and i'll forget i spent the night
tucked in the fetal position
repeat the cycle over and over
numb myself to the world
and let the nightmares spill over

girl in the mirror

who is that?
looking back at me
i don't recognize her face
i think she's me
but infinitely cooler,
confident, and vain
she starts to smile, a devilish grin
filled with sinister seduction
stare into her golden eyes
try to find her soul
but it's not here
nor there, or anywhere
she's just an empty hole

i like me more when she's around
she's who i aim to be
never stays too long though,
it's always a chaotic short-lived stint
but like any deal made with the devil
she comes with terms and conditions
i should have read more carefully,
before i signed my soul on the dotted line
i made a fatal clumsy error,
forgot to read the fine print

now i'm bound by blood
subjected to her sinful reign of terror
i can't have my cake,
and eat it too
i must take the good alongside of the bad
but if i let her overstay her welcome
she will surely drive me mad

our eyes meet once again,
locked into each other's gaze
but if there's any hope
i have to break away,
have to set myself free
suddenly i'm paralyzed
something has a hold on me
i plead and pray
begging to be unchained
i ask her for some mercy
but she likes when i'm in pain

instead, she winks at me
and blows a kiss
then turns to walk away
i wished so badly
for her to leave
but now,
i'm begging her to stay

just a patient

my therapist
became my new best friend
my best gal pal
i felt like more than just
a patient
our relationship was special
she told me i was funny
frequently making her laugh
because my trauma
gave me humor, at least
she understood me
like no one else
and she was always on my side
she knows my story
top to bottom
she's been there from the start
she's seen my light
and she's seen my dark
she let me play the victim,
everyone had wronged me
but with her,
i was always right
things were great
or so i thought

then came a dreadful day
when i realized
the only that she cared
so much
was because i paid her
to make me
feel that way

mixed signals

sometimes "i love you"
can mean "i want to love you"
-i just don't know how

sometimes "i love you"
can mean "i'll stay a little longer"
-maybe things will get better soon

sometimes "i love you"
can mean "i don't know how to leave"
-how do i live without you?

sometimes "i love you"
can mean "i have no one else to turn to
-you are my home

sometimes "i love you"
can mean "i don't know how to love you
in the way that you need to be loved"
-my love language is different than yours

someimes "i love you"
can mean "you mean more to me than air"
-i would give my life for yours

sometimes love can sound like one thing
while meaning something else
sometimes we say it, out of obligation
not realizing
the weight such words carry
and sometimes
we do love someone, with all our heart and being
but we just aren't good at showing it
and that can dilute the meaning

white life raft

my body is sending out
an s.o.s.
it needs someone
to save it,
it's in severe distress
it needs nourished
fed
tended to
with gentle caring hands
but i ignore the smoke signals
turn a blind eye to the fiery flares
instead,
i sit down at my kitchen table
gather my supplies
with a debit card
and a nice clean spoon
i begin to smash and cut
then line up row after row
of perfect powdery white lines
like soldiers standing at attention
getting ready to march
put the straw up to my nose
and take a deep long breath
i cannot help my body

i don't know what to do
but i can quiet down the screaming
the chaos in my head
i'm going numb, feelings muted
my world has just gone silent
and everything
is okay now...
at least
for a little while

distractions

"let me be your distraction"
he hissed
a poisonous snake
hidden in the dark
with venom dripping
from his lips

he strived to be
the one who saved me
from the world and
from myself
he convinced me
to bare my soul to him,
assured me he was
good for my health

he wanted to be
my knight with shining armor
he succeeded in his quest,
leaving me soft, and vulnerable
with exposed organs in my chest
but he never did intend
to keep me
his promised faded away,

his love for me
was just pretend

he distracted me
until a false future together
was all i could see
and then
another damsel in distress
needing his saving
more than me

mania

it's a hot summer night
the middle of july
i crawl in bed at 10pm
and turn off all the lights
pull out my planner
write down all the shit i didn't do
i slam it shut
and use the cover as a table
crush up two pretty white pills
and try to float away
i close my eyes
but cannot sleep, i'm doomed to stay awake
my nerve endings are all exposed
they're raw and they're on fire
i'm restless and i'm bored
a reckless combination
pull out my phone
mass send snapchats
to see who else is up
and of course it's you
i can see you typing back
the conversation heats up fast
my thighs start to tingle
i slide my hand into my pjs

you give me quite a show
tell me that you'll make me cum
and put me right to sleep
but it doesn't
and now you're gone
so i've been staring at the ceiling
birds start chirping
morning sun starts rising
so i rise with it
at 5 am
deciding sleep is overrated
right now seems like the perfect time
to go out
and clean my car

i love him, i love him not

he asked me, "did you love him?"
i chose to answer "no"
i couldn't really love someone
i never got to know.

i want to scream "yes,
i would have died for him!"
i shared with him my secrets
i asked for his in return
but he never said too much
closed right up
and locked the door,
he never let me in.

some days i think i loved him,
other days i'm sure i didn't
it's hard to pick a side
when i don't know where i stand
i want to be rock solid
but i live on unsteady land

i want to give you a straight answer,
a simple yes or no
but neither one feels right,

it's more complicated than that
my brain just flips, it flops around
when it should be standing still
it doesn't have an answer yet,
i don't know if it ever will.
it needs more time to process,
it still needs time to heal.
you can't see my illness,
but i promise you it's there...
would you tell a friend with cancer
that couldn't be true,
because she still had all of her hair?

i wish i could say
we were undoubtedly in love,
our connection written in the stars
it would explain all of my bad behavior
but that's not the truth, it never was
it's so hard to explain
these imaginary scars,
my mind was in an altered state
and clung to him like God,
but he was nothing more
than an attempt at temporary escape...
the only thing he'll ever be to me,
is a devastating mistake.

he didn't love me either,
how could he? i wasn't real
just a disassociated brain and body
floating somewhere out in space,
i wasn't really there at all,
my skin was just aa holding place
maybe it was all a haze,
delusions and hallucinations
courtesy of mania,
kept me trapped, held me captive
they had me in a daze

some of those feelings
had to be real, in the moment at least
but they were phantom pains of love.
only seeing what i wanted to see,
instead of the truth in front of me...
there was no passion,
no commitment,
no blazing fire,
or burning desire.
the reality is much clearer now...
i could never truly love someone,
who was such
a goddamn liar

blocked

instagram
facebook
tiktok
hitting the red button
instead of the blue
snapchat
imessage
i might even block you
on yahoo mail too

not because i despise you
or that i hate seeing your life
in photos and updates
trust me, i'd love to know
"what's on your mind?"
instead, i click confirm
yes, i meant to hit
"i'm sure i want to block this person"
because i know i'm not
what's on your mind,
today anyway

the anxiety
of never knowing

if you'll reach out again
the next time you're bored
or lonely
or horny
or just feel like ruining my life again
knowing damn well
i'd let you

and the pain of knowing
you could reach me,
but just don't want to
shatters me
every time
it crosses my mind

her

spilt in two at birth
separated at the seams
not a twin
but an alter ego
living inside of me
wish i could have
carved *her* out,
a malignant tumor growing
i didn't know
she was cancerous
until she festered
and she spread,
my demons started showing
she became so loud and blaring
gained control over my head
i gave way to *her* demands
let her drag me down to hell
she set me down in the devil's palm
and it was me who
paid the price
for the sins *she* secretly committed
put me in such
a dangerous place
but who is there to blame,

it's hard to tell the difference
her or i,
when we share
the same face

lotto winner

good friends are hard to come by
extremely rare to find
fake people tend to flock to you
when you're not in your right mind

they use you when you're high on drugs
always wanting something from you
and hold your secrets
above their heads
abuse you with their power

snakes hidden in plain sight
but you're too gone to care
so, when you find a good friend
hold on to them and squeeze them tight
praise them like
a fresh breath of air

when last call comes and goes
the lights all turn back on
the coke has all been snorted
the music has stopped playing
and everyone else has gone

they'll be there
with a solid shoulder to cry on
they'll listen when you call
at 4am for no damn reason
they know you like it when they sing
they'll serenade you back to sleep
and check up on you in the morning

that kind of friend
is one in a billion
so please believe me when i say,
treat them like they're the lottery
and you've just won
a hundred million

gemini

you have an affinity
for gossiping, the first to spill the tea
always squawking you hate the drama
yet always seem to be
the epicenter of it

you crave that constant attention
mentally and physically
so, there's always someone new nearby
to satisfy that empty void

you're a charmer too, ya know
always knowing
the right moment
to say the right things
you're stereotyped the flirty one
that's no coincidence

taurus likes to mate for life
but not you, gemini
you're drawn to anything
shiny and new

you love to role play

and dirty talk
the language of sexting
comes easier than english

the zodiac says were incompatible
you're air, i'm water
you move too fast for me

i'm not an expert,
but the quickest way
to break your own heart
is by falling in love
with a fucking
gemini

20. ur fine

am i
borderline?
bipolar?
a combination of the two?
something different entirely?
neither?
are the things i've been through normal?
a rite of passage to growing up,
perfectly normal ways to feel?
i know they aren't,
they can't be...
some days i feel just fine,
i was being overdramatic
it happens all the time
but then my world
turns upside down
flips and flops, gets thrown around
and then i know for sure,
there's something
wrong with me

i woke up feeling sick today
no, it's not a scratchy throat
it's not a cold, and it's not the flu

it's not nearly quite that simple,
not something a handful of nyquil can remedy
something broke
deep inside my brain
it's not a symptom
webmd can explain
if you tell a doctor that your brain has imploded
they'll tell you there's a pill for that
xanax for anxiety, lithium for mood swings
an antihistamine for that pesky insomnia
but the side effects
will take away your dreams
oh, you're feeling suicidal?
we have a padded cell for that
and we'll take you hostage, against your will
force you to join group therapy
and that will help you heal

i'm the girl
who cried there was a wolf
but no one listened, and no one cared
tired of hearing me pout
they only started to believe
when the animal
inside me
had clawed it's way out

21. severed

my demon and i
had a falling out
she got too close
too fast
clung to me
like thick thighs
on leather seats
in the heat of summertime
she wanted commitment
she dreamed of a ring
i was her main chick
but she was only
my side thing
i thought we were better off
as friends
but she couldn't handle rejection
things were getting dicey
the situation becoming dire
i had a choice to make
one of us had to go
i prepared for the looming battle
dusted off my steel-toed boots
pulled out my trusted sword
trained my best horse,

strapped on his armored saddle
i was terrified
she'd kill me dead
she was hungry for my soul
i never wanted it to end like this
but my life was in danger
she made the first move
and left me no choice
but to chop off
her fucking head

www.ingramcontent.com/pod-product-compliance
Lightning Source LLC
LaVergne TN
LVHW050940200726
843508LV00011B/2396